EISENSTAEDT'S CELEBRITY PORTRAITS

EISENSTAEDT'S CELEBRITY PORTRAITS

Fifty Years of Friends and Acquaintances

With an Introduction by Philip B. Kunhardt, Jr.

GREENWICH HOUSE
Distributed by Crown Publishers, Inc.
New York

In army uniform—with a navy cap—while war correspondent in Japan, 1946.

To Alfred
from
Tom

Thomas H. Benton
Jan - 1952

Along the Suez Canal, 1935.

Originally published as *Eisenstaedt's Album*

This 1984 edition is published by Greenwich House, a division
of Arlington House, Inc., distributed by Crown Publishers,
Inc., by arrangement with Viking Penguin Inc.

Manufactured in Japan

Library of Congress Cataloging in Publication Data

Eisenstaedt, Alfred.
Eisenstaedt's celebrity portraits.

Reprint. Originally published: Eisenstaedt's album.
New York, Viking, 1976. (A Studio book)
1. Photography—Portraits.   2. Eisenstaedt, Alfred.
I. Title.
TR680.E32   1984   779′2′0924   83-20712
ISBN: 0-517-433494

Some of my autograph books.

PREFACE

This book, the last in what my publishers like to call the "Eisie trio," differs from *Witness to Our Time* and *People* in that it is the most personal of the three—by far.

The material has been taken not from one album, but from several volumes to which over the years I have kept adding photographs of friends, acquaintances, and places that I have enjoyed and, for one reason or another, knew I would always want to remember.

True to family album tradition, the photographs have been rather haphazardly collected and informally arranged, yet they follow a more or less chronological order from the early 1930s to 1976.

While some of the pictures are of exhibition quality, and have, in fact, been included in various shows, magazines, and books, a few are little more than snapshots, or "snaps"—as it always amuses me to hear those masters of abbreviation, the British, call them. But no matter whether large, small, great, or not so great, like the autographs, sayings, and drawings scribbled around them, each photograph here has a meaning for me, for nostalgic reasons if none other.

It was quite by chance that I started collecting these autographs in the early 1930s. I was in Italy on an assignment for *Die Dame* and was strolling through Florence when, in a shop window along a street near the Ponte Vecchio, my eye was caught by a group of those handsome leather-bound books that the Florentines make so well. As my mission was to photograph some of the dignitaries in that city and in Rome, my companion reporter from *Die Dame* pointed out the possible value of collecting autographs which the editors, she thought, might very likely find interesting to print with the stories we returned with.

Over the years, and particularly on location in Japan in 1945 and 1946 when I saw a display of silk-bound books that tempted me as much as the Florentine ones had, I kept adding to my collection, and, whenever I remembered to do so, I asked the people I was photographing to write in the album I had with me.

I must admit, as I look through these pages once again on their way to the printer, that the number of interesting people and signatures they contain is, with all due modesty, quite remarkable, and sufficiently interesting, I hope, for me to be sharing my album at last with everyone.

On Majorca with Henry R. Luce, founder of Time, Inc.

Caricature by Toombs.

To Kathy and Lucille

ACKNOWLEDGMENTS

My special thanks go to Gael Dillon and Christopher Holme for their design assistance, and to Olga Zaferatos for her invaluable research.

This book would not have been possible without Bryan Holme. For his unflagging devotion in evaluating pictures and autographs to create an interesting layout, I owe him my sincerest gratitude.

To Alfred Eisenstaedt —

I am proud to join the parade of people whom you have made famous — and proudest of all to think that I had a part in starting the parade. And then I must tell you once again — and now for the record — that LIFE ~~owes~~ owes a great debt to you, which you make it easy for us to repay by going along with us with such good cheer. "All thanks and Long Life to Essie"

May 16.'61

Henry R. Luce

In Maryland, after celebrating Dwight
D. Eisenhower's election, 1952.

INTRODUCTION

What do Gloria Vanderbilt, Richard Nixon, Andrew Wyeth, and Gypsy Rose Lee have in common? Or W. H. Auden, Al Capp, and Queen Elizabeth? Or Eddie Fisher, the Shah of Iran, Jonas Salk, and Fannie Hurst? The name game can go on almost forever. Ronald Reagan, Adolf Hitler, Rachel Carson, Stokowski, Chaplin, Ike? Marlene, Marilyn, Barbra, Sophia, Jackie?

The answer—other than fame—is Alfred Eisenstaedt, photographer extraordinary. Eisie for short. He photographed all of them and thousands upon thousands more. Father of photojournalism, he has been called. Has had more pictures published than any other photographer in history. And fame is part of what this small, strong, intense, energetic, durable, inquisitive, naïve, dedicated, and kindly man has been stalking ever since 1929 when, in Berlin, he turned his hobby into his profession by joining the Associated Press as a news photographer. One of the four original photographers for *Life* in 1936, Eisie has, at this writing, completed more than twenty-five hundred assignments all over the world.

In his bag, along with his cameras and lenses and numberless rolls of film, he has always carried, even from the very beginning, a softbound book of blank pages. If he remembers and has time and they are deemed worthy, his subjects, after undergoing the swift, unobtrusive, serious, darting Eisenstaedt scrutiny, are presented the book and asked to add their autographs and any sentiments or comments they might wish to offer. Through the years book after book has been filled—little, tiny, shy handwriting, big scrawls, doodles, drawings, fragments of music, grandiose praise, terse signings, all aimed at saying something to the unique man who had just looked at them through his lens and caught them on film in his precise manner.

His pictures are "wonderful," "magnificent," "superb," "unsurpassed," the autograph books all say in their many different hands. His eye is "sensitive," his heart "generous"; "skilled" he is; "bravo" to him; he is full of "vim and vigor"; "in short," he is, "not bad, not bad at all." Not bad at all is right, as the pages of this book will show. For here, along with the photographs Eisenstaedt took of his famous subjects, many of which never got published—the unguarded moments, the view "just before" or "just after" the event, the very first shot, or the last, the telling scene overlooked by an editor—are reproductions of entries in his autograph books. In a strange way the photographs and the written entries complement each other. Often the subjects felt "tortured," "victims" of the frightening lens that had been recording the secrets of their faces, movements, postures, poses. Anthony Eden called Eisie "the gentle executioner." Others have felt relaxed by the guttural chuckle behind the camera, the murmured words "marvelous" and "incredible" as he worked, the good-tempered simplicity of the man who was trying to define them. "I suppose the people you shoot feel the same way as the people I shoot," wrote a very up-tight Jonas Salk after a tense battle of personalities, the one trying to mask his inner self, the other trying to bring it out on film. "To Alfred Eisenstaedt," wrote President Kennedy after Eisie had taken his official Presidential portrait, "who has caught us all on the edge of the new frontier. What will the passage of the next four years show on his revealing plate?"

At the Time and Life building exhibition of my photographs, "Witness to Our Time," 1966.

Photographing President John F. Kennedy (for his official color portrait) in the Oval Room at the White House, February 26, 1961.

With Kenneth Kaunda before he became President of Zambia.

With Margaret Bourke-White in 1954. At left, photographer Andreas Feininger; at right, Joseph Scherschel.

With actress Celeste Holm in New York.

With Sophia Loren, near Naples, 1961.

A crusty Robert Frost handed Eisie a poem:

> Forget the myth
> There's no one I
> Am put out with
> Or put out by.

Robert Oppenheimer penned a quotation in Greek from Pindar's Third Pythian Ode: "Dear Soul, do not pursue with too much zeal immortal life, but first exhaust the practical mechanics of living." The very next day, after photographing Frank Lloyd Wright, Eisie showed the architect what the physicist had written. With a snort Wright made his own entry: "Take the science of life in your stride as the mechanics of the affair. Art and religion are the essences of being. Cultivate them—they are the payoff."

"Alfred, you make a palace out of my patio," wrote a gracious fledgling of a sexpot in 1953. "But next time," Marilyn Monroe added, "I'd take more time." Of course Marilyn didn't know that speed is one of Eisie's main secrets of success. He is anything but an intellectual photographer. He does not study his subjects for long, or read up on them beforehand, or try to pry into their souls with days and days of shooting. He is instead a reporter with a camera—reporter in an old-fashioned, impartial sense—recording, always recording what is before him and always with speed and directness and taste. Eisie has never had any style particular only to him. One cannot point to a picture on a page and say definitively, "That's an Eisenstaedt," as easily as one can of a Cartier-Bresson or a Gene Smith. Largely that is because he has worked on so many and such varied assignments throughout his career. He has, in fact, done it all, and done it all handsomely—people, places, news, manners, morals, the beautiful, the ugly. But the ugly never as a peddler of gloom; instead, always as a recorder of what is there.

Along with his serious side, Eisie can tickle the funnybone with his pictures. And when the situation warrants, he doesn't mind getting himself into pretty absurd circumstances. For instance, the time he was photographing Gargantua the Gorilla and he wore an automobile tire around his waist for protection in the cage. Or on a 1949 story for *Life* on Hollywood makeup man Wally Westmore. To get into the mood Eisie let himself be made up as Dr. Jekyll's other self, Mr. Hyde. An L. A. correspondent wired the details to the New York office: "Herewith complete list of makeup items Wally Westmore used to make up Eisenstaedt as Mr. Alfred Hyde—forty pounds of plaster of Paris for mold and death mask; one jar Vaseline; one box Kleenex; for modeling on mask two cans undertaker's wax(four pounds); two quarts liquid latex for forehead and nose; one wig; crepe hair; mousseline de soie [soft net fabric used to pull skin]; and also small amounts of face powder, body makeup, eye shadow, etc."

Although Eisie doesn't particularly court danger, he has been known to undergo considerable discomfort to bring back the picture. To get an overall view of the rain forest in Surinam, he was hoisted one hundred and fifty feet into the trees swaying in the wind. And to photograph a hurricane at sea he had himself strapped to the flying bridge of the R.M.S. *Queen Elizabeth* for several hours.

But Eisie usually keeps his feet on the ground. Even though he is quite a technician, no one would ever know it. His technique, which seems so casual, has become instinctive. He has never been a faddist, moving from one school or style of photography to another, or honing away at a special look or shading to his pictures. He doesn't worry his subjects to death. He is an excellent journalist on first look, on first acquaintance. He truly loves what he is doing, every minute of it—that is, when he has a camera in his hand and an assignment in his pocket. Between those times he has been known to scowl, rock back and forth on his toes and heels, purse his lips, grunt, and, in every way he can, make it very evident to his editors that he should be out at work.

Eisenstaedt has a sense of history, an instinct for the moment. The pictures that follow attest to this, as well as do the scribbled words of affection, praise, and awe. Always something comes out of Eisie's camera good enough to fill books. Now, here is one, not only out of his camera, but from the books in his camera bag as well.

—Philip B. Kunhardt, Jr.

The man with a Leica face.

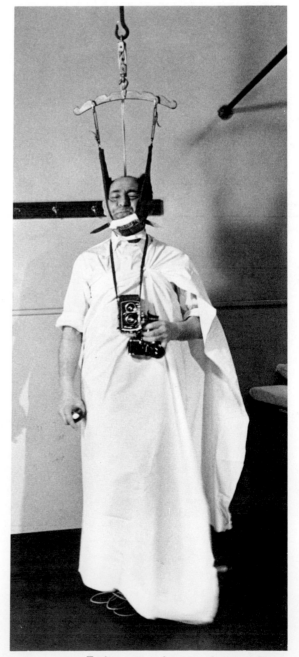

Trying out a harness for stretching neck muscles while photographing a story on arthritis.

At a zoo in Illinois.

Wally Westmore, the Hollywood makeup artist, showed me how different I could look!

As Veronica Lake—with Bob Hope.

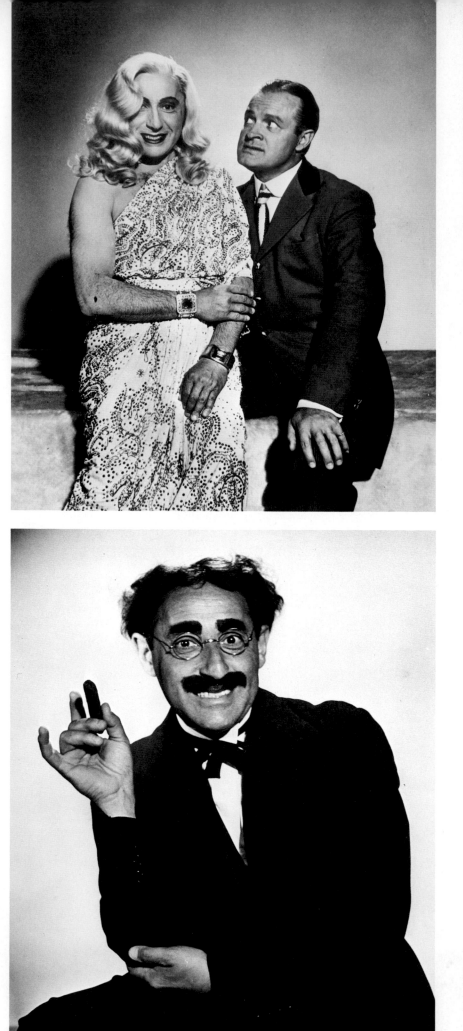

As Mr. Hyde.

As Groucho Marx.

Opposite: As Napoleon Bonaparte.

George Bernard Shaw in London, 1932.

The *Graf Zeppelin* at Pernambuco, Brazil, 1933.

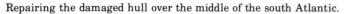

Repairing the damaged hull over the middle of the south Atlantic.

A passenger shows card tricks to Count von Eckner, a co-developer of the *Graf Zeppelin*. Center: Hans von Schiller, deputy commander of the *Graf Zeppelin*. Right: Captain Lehmann with his accordion.

Luftschiff „Graf Zeppelin"
V. Südamerikafahrt 1933.
Ernst A. Lehmann
29. VIII. 33.

Crew quarters inside the hull.

Captain Ernst A. Lehmann, who later commanded the *Hindenburg*.

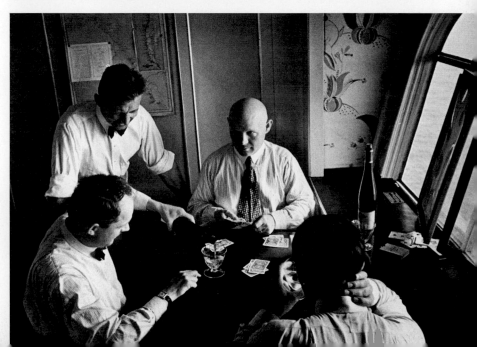

Engineers off duty.

Zur frdl. Erinnerung an Frz Kreisler 21. Juli 1937

Freundliche Grüsse u herzlichen Dank für die prachtvollen Bilder. Willem Mengelberg.

The German author Jakob Wassermann.

Jakob Wassermann

Fritz Kreisler in Berlin.

Adoro l'arte della
fotografia e perciò sono
specialmente lieto di aver
conosciuto un così egregio
artista. Nicola Benois
Milano
Scala 23/XII-33

Alexandre Benois finishing a backdrop at La Scala, Milan, 1933.

Willem Mengelberg leading the Concert-
gebouw Orchestra in Amsterdam, 1932.

Carl Milles at the Cranbrook Academy, 1937.

Crown Prince Gustav Adolf and Princess Louise of Sweden, 1934.

Louise
Kronprinzessin von Schweden

Nobel Prize winner Niels Bohr (right) working at an atom-smashing device in Copenhagen.

Mme. A. Kollontay—friend of Lenin and Soviet Ambassador to Denmark, 1934.

Niels Bohr
Professor Universitet Kopenhagen
19-4-1938

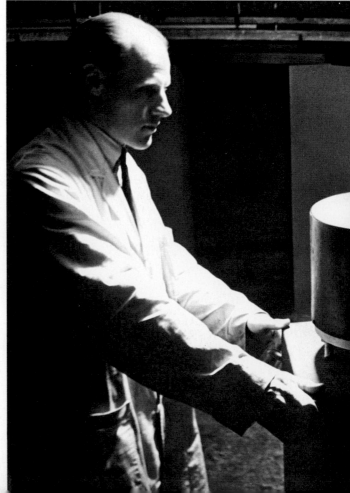

Kronprinz von Schweden.
Smyrna "Vasaland".
Oct. 12. 1934.

King Gustav V of Sweden.

Stockholm 12/5 1934.

In Venice, 1934. Left to right: Bodyguard for Hitler; Adolf Hitler; Ulrich von Hassel, German Ambassador to Italy who was later executed by Hitler; Benito Mussolini; and, with arm raised in fascist salute, Count Cerutti, Italian Ambassador to Germany.

Blomberg

Werner von Blomberg, Commander of the Reichswehr. Above him hangs a portrait of Hermann Göring.

Princess Olga of Yugoslavia.

The Imperial seal of Ethiopia.

Paul
Prinz Regent von Jugoslawien
12. XII. 34
Belgrad

Prince Paul of Yugoslavia.

Emperor Haile Selassie shortly before
the Italian invasion of Ethiopia, 1935.

Agnes
1935 -
Paris novembre.

Robert Piguet
Paris 26 novembre 1935

M Rochas

Je souhaite que l'homme
aimable et l'artiste que vous
êtes trouve une hospitalité
bienveillante et le succès
dans ce voyage vers le monde
nouveau.

alix

Top row: Hattie Carnegie, Robert Piguet, Alix, Mr. John, Elizabeth Arden.

Center, left: Marcel Rochas; left: Mme. Agnes watching Countess von Hohenlohe trying on a hat.

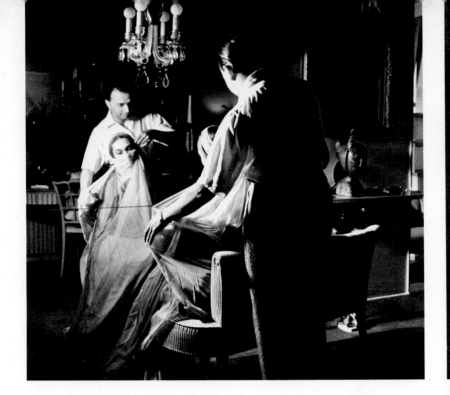

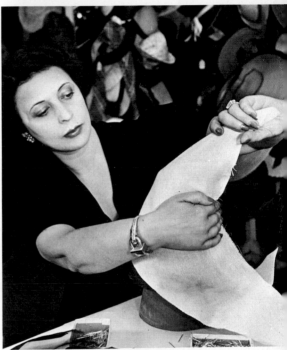

after Rubinstein does two
faces — I do the rest
Elizabeth Arden
April 193
New York

Hattie Carnegie

En toute jalousie
un confrère admiratif
Lucien Vogel
24 Novembre 1935
La Faisanderie. Asnières.-

Center, right: Lily Daché; right:
Helena Rubinstein.

Helena Rubinstein

Gloria Swanson with her husband, Michael Farmer, in St. Moritz, 1933.

*Louis Barthou
ministre des Affaires Étrangère
Genève, 1er juin 1934*

Jean Louis Barthou, France's Foreign Minister, in 1934. A few months later he and King Alexander of Yugoslavia were assassinated in Marseilles.

*Dem Meister des
Lichtbildes Alfred Eisenstaedt
Gerhart Hauptmann
1934*

Right: Gerhart Hauptmann and Mrs. Hauptmann with prodigy violinist Ruggiero Ricci. Berlin, 1934.

Richard Strauss (with hat) in Salzburg, 1931.

Marlene Dietrich and Anna May Wong. Berlin, 1928.

Arturo Toscanini in Bayreuth.

TO ALFRED EISENSTADT
MY BEST
WISHES
Walt Disney

HOLLYWOOD 1936

Walt Disney, 1936.

ctress Luise Rainer with Dr. Arme
auritzen. St. Moritz, 1932.

Mariette Lydis.

Vincente Minnelli, then stage designer 1936.

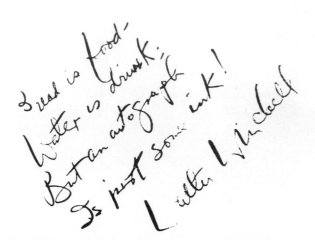

Walter Winchell, the columnist, 1936.

Fred Allen. Even comedians have serious moments. 1936.

Choreographer and founder of the American Ballet, George Balanchine.

Ruth Slenczynski New York Oct. 27, 1936

Pianist Ruth Slenczynski with Radio City Music Hall conductor Erno Rapée, 1936.

Henry R. Luce and Clare Boothe Luce—
eight months after their marriage. 1936.

To Alfred Eisenstaedt
who confers on most of
us what little perishable
permanence we will have
in the annals of our
times.
With admiration
Clare Boothe Luce

Rudy Vallee.

Sinclair Lewis rehearsing one of his plays, 1936.

Best wishes
Helen Hayes
New York
Oct 26, 1936

She lives in my building, too!
(And nothing ever happens!)

N.Y. City!
Rudy Vallée. *Oct. 25.*

Eugene Talmadge, Governor of Georgia.

Helen Hayes going over a script.

olo player Thomas Hitchcock, 1938.

Alice Marble with Daniel Long-
well, executive editor of *Life*.

Katharine Hepburn modeling the hat she wore
in the film *The Philadelphia Story*.

At Sun Valley, Idaho.

Mr. and Mrs. Averell Harriman.

Melvyn Douglas.

Claudette Colbert

Sun Valley – Idaho –
Feb 8 – 1937

Robert Young
I aspire to your
perfection in photography.
"
Melvyn Douglas – 1936
Sun Valley

Claudette Colbert with Robert Young during the filming of *I Met Him in Paris*

Mickey Rooney and Irving Berlin at Franklin D. Roosevelt's inauguration festivities, Washington, D.C., 1941.

I hope you get a good one — If not
kink blame me — I did everything you
said — Many thanks and best wishes

Irving Berlin
Your Pal
Mickey Rooney

For Alfred.
It was a real joy to work with a true artist — I am sincerely grateful.

Sincerely
John Garfield

P.S. I knew to be a flop!

John Garfield.

To Alfred,
who can make even
a long photographic sitting seem
attractive!!!
With my sincere thanks.
Madeleine Carroll.
Malibu. September . 1938.

Madeleine Carroll in Hollywood after her success in Alfred Hitchcock's English film *The Thirty-Nine Steps*.

For Alfred —
With my every best
wish   Thank you.
Sincerely,
Tyrone Power

Tyrone Power.

Ronald Colman.

To sincere appreciation
+ wishing you the very
best — always
Ronald Colman
Sept. 1938.

James Stewart and Carole Lombard.

To Alfred Guirot —
you are truly —
In sincere appreciation
always
Carole Lombard.
—1938.

Carole Lombard.

Cecil B. De Mille stretching his muscles.

*Greetings from Hollywood
to Alfred Eisenstaedt
Cecil B. deMille.
New York City — January 15 — 1938*

Hedy Lamarr with image of herself, 1938.

Jane Froman waiting for a rehearsal to begin, 193

*To Alfred
A Master — with the
camera — hope I have
the pleasure of sitting
for you again
Hedy Lamarr
Hollywood Oct — 1938.*

Best wishes, Alfred.

*Reginald
Gardiner.*

To Alfred
Eisenstadt – for
whose artistry I have
a great admiration
Eddie Cantor

To Alfred. –
one of the few fellows
that held me still for
more than 1/2 of a second.
Jack L. Warner
Sept 22 – 1938.

Bette Davis, 1938.

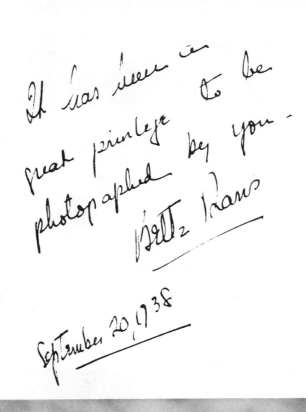

It has been a great privilege to be photographed by you.

Betty Evans

September 20, 1938

ack Warner, the brains behind Warner Bros.

To Alfred —

With my utmost appreciation for your lovely work — Best regards always

Loretta Young

Loretta Young.

Barbara Stanwyck at Marwyck Ranch, 1938.

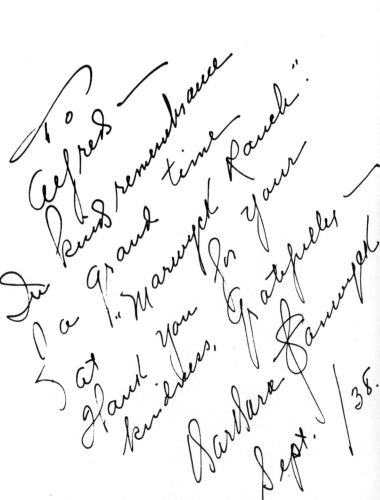

Shirley Temple—the dimpled darling of Hollywood, 1936.

To
Alfred —
In kind remembrance
of a grand time
at "Marwyck Ranch."
Thank you for your
kindness. Gratefully —
Barbara Stanwyck
Sept. 1/38.

Josef Hofmann in his workshop.

To Alfred

Love,

Shirley Temple

May everything always be F.Q. at a 50th
It's not what you shoot but how you do it

Mortimer gets his teeth polished by ventriloquist Edgar Bergen.

Edgar Bergen

Joan Crawford.

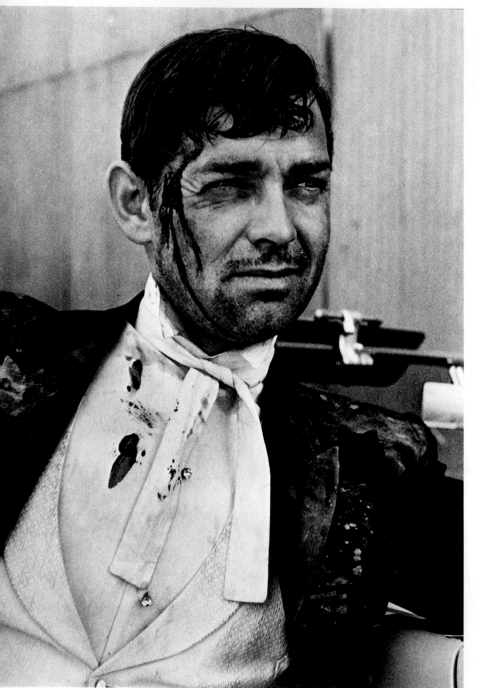

On the set with Clark Gable.

Opposite: Marlene Dietrich lunching at the canteen.

Jonas Lie.

To Alfred Eisensta[edt]
in gratitude and
high esteem
[?] Yours [?]

New York, Friday Oct. 13..

John Steuart Curry.

Thomas Hart Benton.

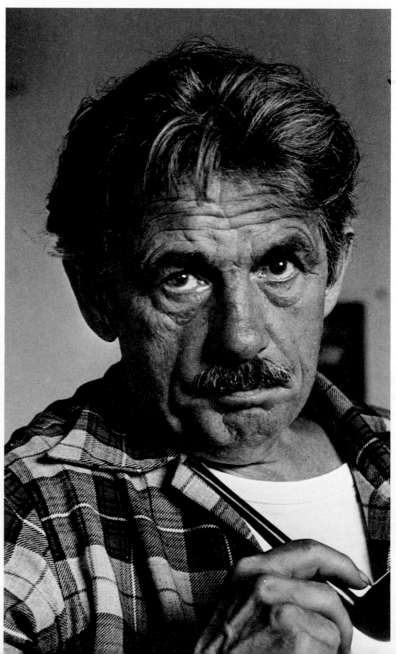

Jackson Pollock with friends.

To a splended artist
with all good wishes

RE Byrd

Boston, sept. 1939.

Admiral Richard Byrd shortly before his Antarctic expedition.

To Alfred

Kate Smith in 1938.

Hildegarde at the Plaza's Persian Room, New York.

To Alfred, —
May all your
dark rooms have
silver linings
good luck
Nelson Eddy
1938

Marian Anderson
Philadelphia
Penna
May 27th, 1938

Marian Anderson singing at the Academy of Music, Philadelphia.

Mar. 17 - 1939 -

To Alfred:
It has indeed
been a rare privilege to be
your subject today — You have
been so patient and kind — that we
must have some good ones? yes?
I hope I will have the pleasure
to be photographed by you many many
more times to come —
May you derive much Happiness
and good fortune in your magnificent
artistry
Sincerely
Hildyard

The publishing team of Simon and Schuster—
Richard L. Simon (left) and Max L. Schuster.

Christopher Morley, while his novel *Kitty Foyle* was still on the best-seller list.

If Alfred Eisenstaedt
          played cricket —
He'd bowl the ball
          right at the wicket:
His art is greater than
                    other men's —
He bowls the light
          Right through the lens.
Alfred! No matter how you
                    tricked your
Sitter, you got a Perfect Picture!

With affectionate greetings, here at the
Germantown Cricket Club, Feb 23, McMXL
          Christopher Morley

Roy E. Larsen, President of Time, Inc.

With great respect
and admiration
M Lincoln Schuster

To Alfred Eisenstadt
who can boss me around
anywhere anytime he wants
to my honor
Roy E. Larsen
Dec 14 '39

Thanking Alfred Eisenstaedt
for his patience, his courtesy,
his genius and his art.
            A.H. Vandenberg
Washington, January 19. 1939.
            #

Senator Arthur H. Vandenberg of Michigan.

Secretary of State Cordell Hull, 1937.

Whittaker Chambers, *Time* magazine's Foreign Affairs editor.

Cordell Hull
Apr. 21, 1937.

Opposite: Wendell Willkie campaigning against Franklin D. Roosevelt in New Jersey, 1940.

Louis Bromfield.

Louis Bromfield

Joan Blondell and Ralph Glover in *The Naked Genius*, 1943.

For Alfred
    who makes being photographed
almost endurable —

        Dorothy Thompson.
    August 29 - Barnard Vt

Dorothy Thompson.

with my best wishes
to Alfred Eisenstaedt

— Edna St. Vincent Millay

New York, March 3, 1941

Edna St. Vincent Millay.

So now I
know about "apple
— Thanks, to You —
All that's good —
Joan Blondell

The Kennedys at Hyannisport, Massachusetts, 1940.

Opposite: Rose, Teddy, and Kathleen.

Michèle Morgan rehearsing.

I hope you had as much fun as I had, taking those pictures! Kindly, Michèle Morgan Oct 5th 3. 42

To Alfred Eisenstaedt and his wise wonderful unforgiving cameras — Thank you for a very nice afternoon. Dorothy McGuire October 194

Dorothy McGuire.

Early-morning training at Belmont Park.

June Harrah adding the final touch.

Horsebreeder Alfred Gwynne Vanderbilt
in his Belmont Park office.

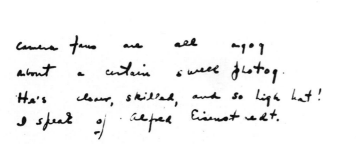

...'s a grand person

Give X *rough*

1943

Roy Rogers and his palomino Trigger.

Camera fans are all agog
about a certain swell photog.
He's clever, skilled, and so high hat!
I speak of Alfred Eisenstaedt.

His photographs have so much glamor
That amateurs can only stammer.
attempts to imitate this feat.
There's only one A. Eisenstaedt.

Maggie Bourke-White

Time & Life Bldg.
N.Y.C. July 20 '42.

Margaret Bourke-White.

Oscar Serlin, Teresa Wright, and Sam Jaffe reading a Ferenc Molnar script. Rockport, Massachusetts, 1941.

W. Somerset Maugham, 1

Nelson Doubleday at home in South Carolina.

With best regards,
Ferenc Molnár
Gloucester, Mass. 1941

Ferenc Molnar.

May your shadows
never grow less!
Nelson Doubleday
Bonny Hall
April 12th 1942

J. Frank Dobie, author of *The Longhorns*.

Branded for
Alfred Eisenstaedt —
while he takes my
picture —
J. Frank Dobie

Austin Tex.
July 6, 1943

Mr. Eisenstaedt's a swell
photographer, but he's never
satisfied — his clients are,
tho — 'etis callit a day

Sept 2[?]

Ha dim Litvinoff
Washington D.C.
Sept. 30th 1942

s Foreign Minister Maxim Litvinov with his wife, Ivy.

for good luck Krylenko
Eliena Krylenko
Gay Head
Oct. 1944

Pictures are more effective
than books, one finds;
Eyes are so much more
open than minds.

Max Eastman

Max Eastman and Mrs. Eastman (Eliena Krylenko).

At Broadway's Zanzibar nightclub, 1944:

Milton Berle.

Jackie Gleason.

Bill "Bojangles" Robinso

Kathy on our wedding day, June 24, 1949.

One of Kathy's typical notes to me.

*Every morning I send
You a loving thought
and a gentle kiss
to send you on
Your way*

Katinka

Alicia Markova in Antony Tudor's ballet *The Pillar of Fire*.

With best wishes
Lauritz Melchior
Metropolitan Opera

Lauritz Melchior, shortly before giving his
two hundredth performance as Tristan at the
Metropolitan Opera House, 1944.

Marjorie Lawrence preparing herself as
Venus in Wagner's *Tannhäuser*.

In remembrance
+ best wishes
Grace Moore
Jan. 1944

Gladys Swarthout.

To Alfred
The most wonderful
and famous of
all photographers
Most cordially
Gladys Swarthout
November 15th '44

Soprano Grace Moore with Prince Serge Obolensky.

Lord Keynes *leader of*
British Delegation

Henry Morgenthau Jr.
Bretton Woods
July 3rd 1944.

Lord Keynes and Secretary of the Treasury Henry Morgenthau at the Bretton Woods Monetary Conference, 1944.

To Mr Eisenstaedt from his
victim the long suffering
Thomas Barbour

M. C. Z.
Harvard U.
Camb.
Mass.

Thomas Barbour and stuffed friends at Harvard.

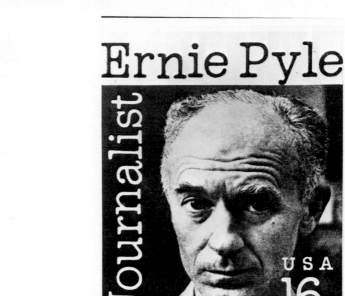

To Alfred —
— (in Jo Davidson's studio) — of course I
haven't seen the pictures yet since you're just now
taken them, but if they're as understanding as your
presence while taking them (which of course they will be)
then they will please us all —
— Ernie Pyle.

Sept. 20, 1944

Ernie Pyle, Helen Keller, and Jo Davidson in the sculptor's studio, 1944.

George Jessel and Leonard Lyons share a mutual friend (between them) at the Stork Club, 1944.

Leonard Lyons

At the Seven Arts Ball in 1944:

Mrs. Stuart Rhinelander with Bayard Swope.

Mr. and Mrs. James Farley.

Mr. and Mrs. (Eleanor Holm) Billy Rose.

Mrs. Lytle Hull, Cole Porter, and Elsa Maxwell.

Odgen Pleissner.

Mar 1945

To Alfred with Best wishes
Ogden - Pleissner

Floyd Davis.

Pisa - 1944

For Alfred Eisenstaedt
Edward Laning

Edward Laning.

David Fredenthal.

A picture of a great artist for Alfred

March, 1945, N.Y.C.

best regards

David Fredenthal

To Alfred Eisenstaedt
— on a whole day
shadowing the G.M. before the
opening in 1946.

Arte è lunga
La vita è corta!

Cordially

Edward Johnson

12.4. 1946

With my appreciation
and admiration
Lily Pons

Edward Johnson, general manager of the Metropolitan Opera, with, above, Margaret Truman and, left, Lily Pons, star of *Lakmé*, the opera that opened the 1946 season at the Met.

Emperor Hirohito inspecting bomb damage near Tokyo, 1946.

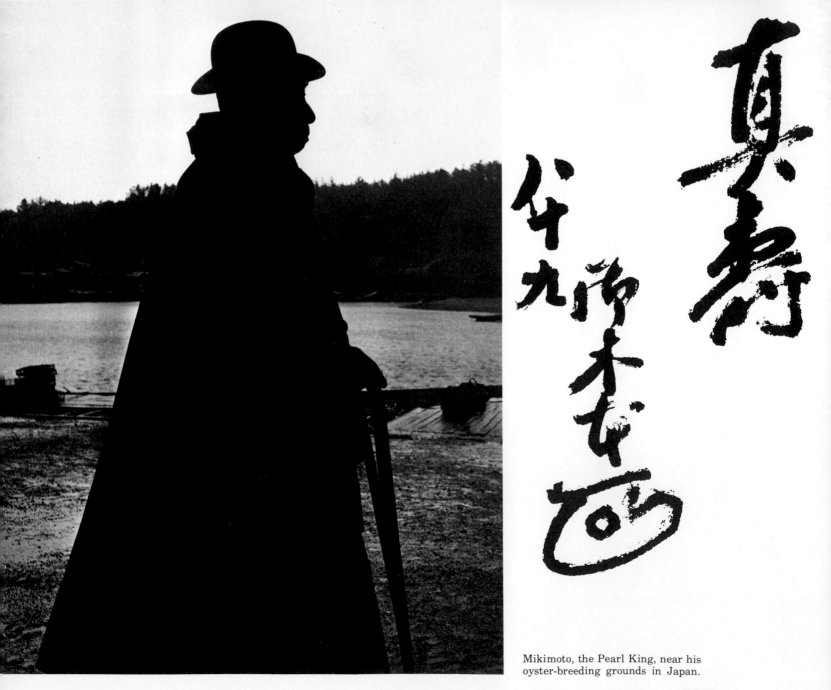

真寿

八十九 御木本幸吉 画

Mikimoto, the Pearl King, near his oyster-breeding grounds in Japan.

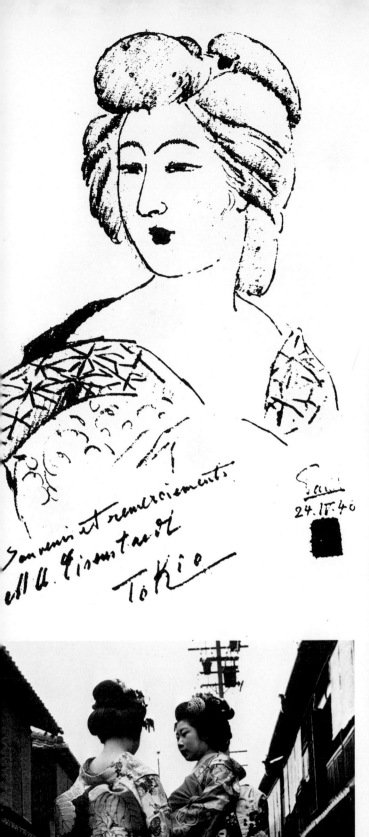

Souvenir et remerciements
M.M. Eisenstaedt
Tokio
Paul
24.IV.40

Paul Yacqoulet exhibits one of his woodcuts.

Geishas in Kyoto.

There is none who could not be moved by sincerity.

Kichisaburo Nomura
mar. 5th 1946.
Tokio

General Douglas MacArthur, in the autographed photograph he presented to me.

With best wishes to Alfred Eisenstaedt

Douglas MacArthur

Tokyo - 1946.

With special Japanese envoy Kichisaburu Nomura.

At the indictment of Japanese war criminals in Tokyo, 1946. General Hideki Tojo, Premier of Japan, is at center (with mustache).

Edgar Snow, friend of Mao Tse-tung.

To Alfred Eisenstadt, who
has saved many a man's
face — a very superior
occupation, according to
Confucius. With much
appreciation —
Edgar Snow

Tokyo,
Japan, 1946

Mr. and Mrs. John Kenneth Galbraith in the early 1950s.

William Carlos Williams.

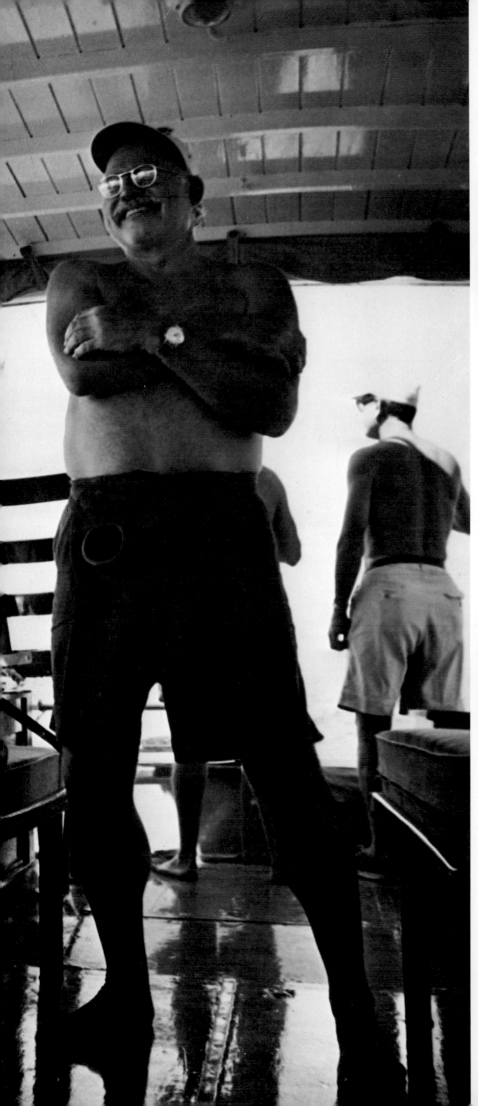

wishing him all good luck always and for all of his life

Ernest Hemingway

Ernest Hemingway on his deep-sea fishing boat near Morro Castle; and, above, with his wife, Mary, at the Royal Yacht Club, Havana, 1953.

Josef Beran, Archbishop of Prague.

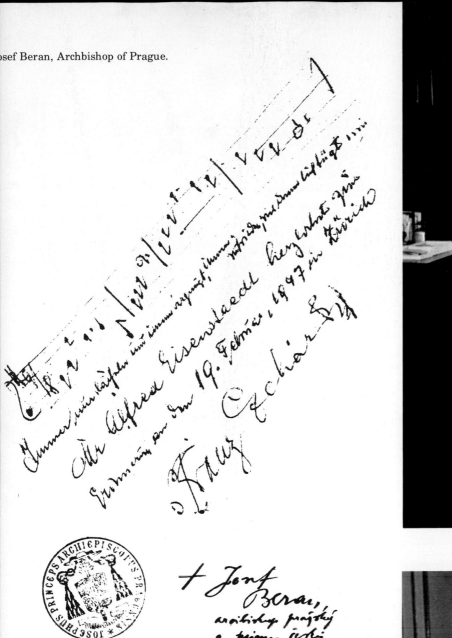

Franz Lehár and wife, Nellie, 1947.

President Eduard Beneš of Czechoslovakia at the Hradshani Palace, Prague.

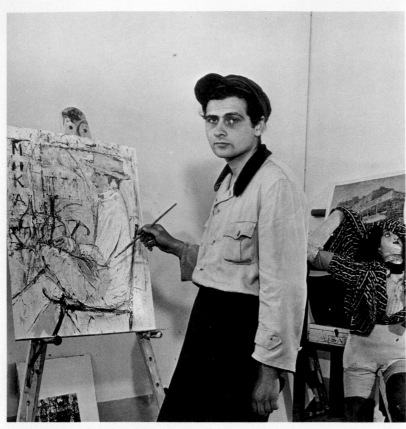

Renzo Vespignani in his Rome studio.

A Alfred Eisenstaedt
con amicizia
Vespignani 1947
Roma - Maggio.

I like folks who know how.
Alfred Eisenstaedt is certainly
one of them.

Good luck to him

from

Jan Masaryk

Prague - March 22-19...

Jan Masaryck, Czechoslovakia's Foreign Minister,
in 1947. A year later he was killed by the Nazis.

King Peter II and Queen Alexandra of Yugoslavia, St. Moritz, 1947.

Pablo Picasso's signature.

A Mr. Alfred Eisenstaedt
Picasso

With best wishes to
Mr. Alfred Eisenstaedt
St Moritz 1947.
Peter II. Alexandra R.

Salvador Dali with friend in 1947.

1947

A royal dinner party, given by Prince Abdel Montim of Egypt at the Palace Hotel, St. Moritz. The guests (clockwise from left foreground) are: Greek diplomat Taky Corvissiano; the Princess of Hesse; Prince Nicholas of Rumania; the hostess; Prince Christian of Hesse; Princess of Schaumburg-Lippe; Baron Charles de Buxhoeveden; Peter Zervudachi of Greece; M. de la Huera, Spanish Embassy Secretary in Paris; Princess Nicholas; the host; Princess Sixte de Bourbon-Parme; Belgian Marquis D'Assche; and Austrian Baron Doblhoff.

Place Vendôme, Paris.

J. Robert Oppenheimer, teaching at Princeton (above), and (below) hurrying home, wearing his trademark: the pork-pie hat. Right, with Albert Einstein, 1947.

Der Teufel scheisst auf den grossen Haufen.

A. Einstein.
Nov 47.

To Eisenstadt — for this latest attempt to record men in their most difficult act: thinking greetings —

Robert Oppenheimer

Princeton
November 1947

To Alfred Eisenstaedt —
With all good wishes —
Jascha Heifetz

It was a pleasure
to be tortured ~~over~~,
~~by~~ taking for endless
hours pictures of me.!
God bless you.
Dimitri Mitropoulos
Jan. 25. 1945. Minneapolis
Minnesota

Dimitri Mitropoulos conducting Jascha Heifetz and the Minneapolis Symphony Orchestra in William Walton's Violin Concerto.

*R. M. S. "Queen Elizabeth"
at Sea.
Jan. 19. 1948.*

Mr. Alfred Eisenstaedt stood on the bridge of this vessel in one of the worst storms yet encountered for several hours, clad in gum boots and oilskin, waiting for the split second in which to get the North Atlantic and the Queen meeting with a "Smack".

Best wishes to the intrepid photographer!

Yours

*Chas. M. Ford.
Master*

Aboard the S.S. *Queen Elizabeth* with the ship's master, Captain Charles M. Ford.

*Happiness is the absence of pain.
"Retouching" is the absence of beauty!*

Sayings of Paulette Goddard

For Alfred Eisenstaedt who knows

Burgess Meredith and his wife, Paulette Goddard.

Hurricane in the Atlant

For Alfred Eisenstaedt

Dec. 19, 1949
N.Y.C.

Mr. John creates a hat for Celeste Holm, 1950.

Even our dog Tish
loved you at once.
With gratitude
Nina Koshetz

Nina Koshetz, the Russian soprano, with Efrem Kurtz.

You certainly know
how to win friends.
At least, you won
me and Mrs Carnegie

May you always
have fair winds
and sunny skies.

Dale Carnegie

To Alfred Eisenstaedt
who has raised me
high above my
station by asking
me to put my
name at the tail end
of such great, good
people —
I'm thanking you

Hedda Hopper
July — 3 — 1949

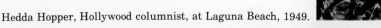
Hedda Hopper, Hollywood columnist, at Laguna Beach, 1949.

etty Grable and Victor Mature on the set of *Wabash Avenue*.

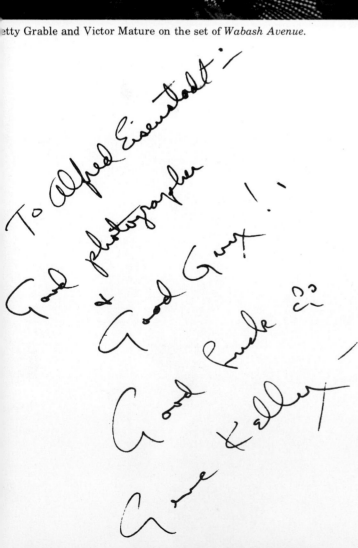

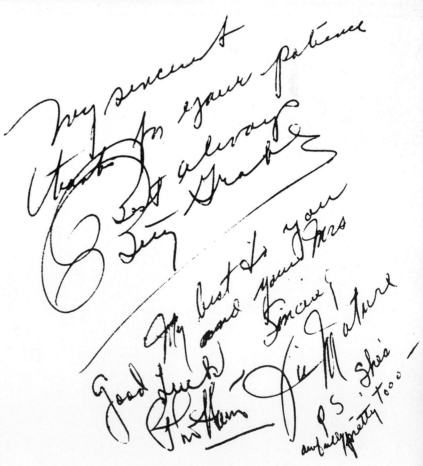

Lauren Bacall and Kirk Douglas during
the filming of *Young Man with a Horn*.

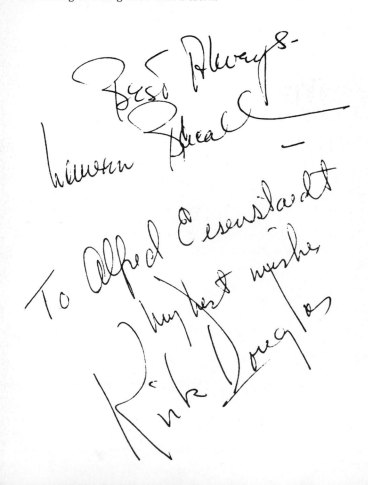

Bob Hope.

Betty Hutton and Fred Astaire in *Let's Dance*.

All best wishes
Danny Kaye

The Best
Bob Hope
July 27-'49

Dame Ninette de Valois, director of the Sadler's Wells Ballet (now The Royal Ballet), with members of the company. London, 1951.

For Alfred Eisenstaedt —

Hugh Casson
Nov 14. 1951.
London —

Giles Gilbert Scott, studying his designs of the Liverpool Cathedral,

Ninette de Valois
Nov. 1957

Giles Gilbert Scott
Nov. 1957

Opposite: Sir Hugh Casson.

Bertrand Russell.

S. Eliot.

Joyce Cary.

To/
Alfred Eisenstaedt
the acrobatic photographer,
with apologies for giving
him such a difficult
job.
T. S. Eliot
19. xi. 51

one does not suffer to be
fairly beautiful

Oxford 11. 13. 51   Joyce Cary

Benjamin Britten listening while his *Peter Grimes* is recorded at Covent Garden Opera House.

Sir David Low, the famous British cartoonist, 1951.

David LOW
1951

Augustus Joh

To Alfred
Eisenstaedt
of the seeing eye.

Charles Laughton

May 14th 1952

Charles Laughton.

Lord Beaverbrook (William Maxwell Aitken), owner of London's *Daily Express* and *Evening Standard*.

Christopher Fry, 1951.

This is my vision:
what will yours be?

Christopher Fry

November 10. 1951

Britain's foremost Jesuit scholar, The
Very Reverend Martin Cyril D'Arcy.

To

my companion for
many days—
And therefore my
friend

Beaverbrook

with "Mind & Heart"
& best wishes for the series in
England   Martin C. D'Arcy J

Tallulah Bankhead.

Dame Edith Evans filming *The Importance of Being Earnest.*

Alec Guinness, 195

A cocktail party at the Breakers Hotel, Newport, Rhode Island, at the finale of the America's Cup Races, 1958.

Warm good wishes and thanks for a happy session at Boston. Jan. 29. 1952
Emlyn Williams

Soprano Risë Stevens.

In the future I will always think of birds and cranes when I have a photo taken. "Apples too!"
Many thanks —
Risë Stevens

May 19, 1954

Emlyn Williams as Hamlet, 1952.

Following a Royal Command Performance of the film *Where No Vultures Fly,* Queen Elizabeth and the Duke of Gloucester commend Dame Margaret Rutherford for her performance. Next to the Queen is the Duchess of Kent, speaking with actress Merle Oberon.

Merle Oberon.

Comedian Bert Lahr plays umpire.

Zoologist Konrad Lorenz.

Civil-rights leader Martin Luther King, Jr., with Kenneth
Kaunda (later President of Zambia) in Atlanta, 1960.

To
Mr. Alfred Eisenstaedt
(Eisie to his friends)

with the best regards of one
who wishes he could photograph half as well!

Konrad Lorenz

Truman Capote dictating his impressions at
the Rockefeller Center ice-skating rink, 1959.

For A. E. (my favorite ice-skating
Companion); "Je Responderay" —
Truman Capote. 1959

With my thanks for a relatively painless operation

Henry H. Dale

Sir Henry H. Dale, Nobel Prize laureate in Physiology and Medicine.

Secretary of Defense George C. Marshall, 1950.

Eleanor Roosevelt with the Shah of Iran, at Hyde Park, 195

Mohammad-Reza Pahlavi

To Mr. Eisenstaedt with recollections of a pleasant day spent on November 29th 1954 in Hyde Park.

Eleanor Roosevelt

Sir Winston Churchill in his library at Chartwell, Kent, and, right, arriving at 10 Downing Street, following his appointment as Prime Minister.

Winston S. Churchill

1951

October.

For Alfred
Eisenstaedt
a gentle executioner
with every good wish
from

Anthony Eden

Anthony

a fruitful fellow
CRA
1.4.52

Clement Attlee, leader of England's Labor Party, arriving by ship in New York.

Otto Preminger directing *The Thirteenth Letter*, 1951.

Harold Stassen (hatless) campaigning
in the New Hampshire primary, 1952.

Dear Al, if you'll like the
"Scarlet Pen" as much as we of
the "Scarlet Pen" to be for you
we have nothing to worry about.

Montreal, Oct. 1950   Cordially,
                        Otto Preminger

To Alfred Eisenstaedt
Incomparable artist
who always gets his man!
Even in New Hampshire!
        Best of luck always!
        Harold Stassen

Charles Boyer in *The Thirteenth Letter*

with greetings from
Rocky New Hampshire

Sherman Adams
Gov.
195—

Sherman Adams (center left), Eisenhower's Chief of Staff, at the 1952 Republican Convention, Chicago.

with best wishes

Dwight D. Eisenhower

Vice-President Richard M. Nixon in Guatemala, 1955.

with pleasant memories of our trip to Central America and with best wishes for good living, good luck, and the best pictures! — in the years ahead — from

Richard Nixon
February 7, 1955

Opposite: Dwight D. Eisenhower during his inauguration parade, January 20, 1953. Mamie Eisenhower smiles at right.

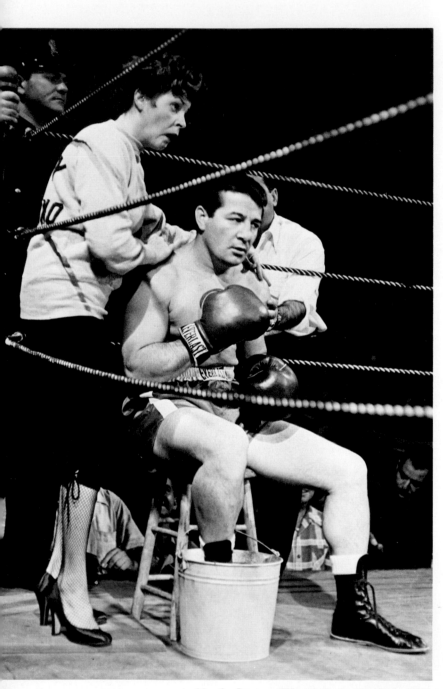

Martha Raye on TV with Rocky Graziano, 1953.

"Relax and the world is beautyfull and who can make you relax better than Mr. Eisendaedt! Thank you

Shirley Booth

May 28 1953

yril Ritchard, allowing his ermine to be in-
pected, and a distraught Joan Greenwood
eft) in the TV production *The King and
'rs. Candle.*

hirley Booth offstage with Mimi.

Debbie Reynolds and Eddie Fisher at their wedding reception, 1955.

Alfred
You made a picture
out of my pants —
But next time let
to take ..... more Time
Love, Marilyn Monroe
June 1953.

Marilyn Monroe in Hollywood, 1953.

Lillian Gish in her New York apartment.

This for remembrance.
And looking to the future
Only the best to you
Lillian Gish

Boris Artzybasheff, book illustrator and magazine artist.

ink admiration and many thanks for his patience.

W. H. Auden
Jan 25th. 1955.

W. H. Auden reading his poetry in 1955.

Dr. Jonas Salk.

I now know the reason for the kind things said to you and about you. I can add that you are the first photographer whom I did not resent. I would like to meet you when you do not have the camera. Only then could I be relaxed. I suppose the people I "shoot" feel the same way as those you "shoot".

Jonas E. Salk

To Alfred Eisenstaedt — the great photographer of men and birds in their natural habitat

Boris Artzybasheff

Bess Truman.

Former President Harry Truman, father of the bride.

Clifton Daniel with the former Margaret Truman on the day they were married, April 21, 1956.

With kind regards to
Alfred Eisenstaedt
from
Harry Truman
Independence
Nov. 17, 1955

Truman back from his customary six A.M. walk.

Lionel Trilling in 1956, shortly after writing *The Opposing Self*.

To Alfred Eisenstaedt
with my gratitude ...
for the pleasantest photographic
sitting I have ever had,
and in high admiration
of his art. Lionel Trilling
15 May 1956

Hands across the Years!
Wonderful to see you again —
with all the vim and vigor
of your artistry, intact —
or rather on the plus side.
Fannie Hurst
1959

Elaine Pojade teaching Fannie Hurst how to paint in 1959.

Sidney Hook of New York University, 1952.

To Alfred Einsenstaedt as great artist and warm human being from whom I learned that good judgment is good taste in photography as in other things

Sidney Hook

May 17 '52

Jacques Maritain.

To Alfred Eisenstaedt
with my gratitude for his kindness
and my admiration for his art
Cordially,
Jacques Maritain

Leonard Bernstein in rehearsal.

Judy Garland partying at the Gilbert Millers'.

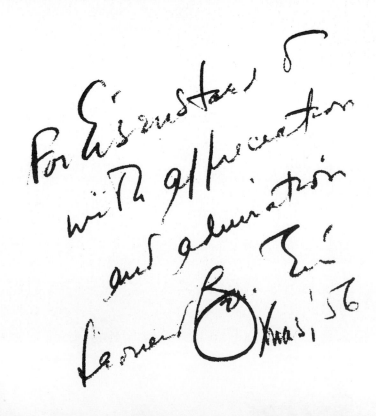

For Eisenstaedt
with affection
and admiration
Leonard Bernstein Xmas '56

Queen Elizabeth II and the Duke of Edinburgh. Opposite, with Mr. and Mrs. John Foster Dulles.

The Greek Royal Family: Queen Frederika, Princess Sophia (now Queen of Spain), and Constantine, Duke of Sparta (later King Constantine), in 1955.

The Duke and Duchess of Windsor.

Alexander Calder with Gian Carlo Menotti in 1958.

Robert Frost at a seminar in Breadloaf, Vermont (1958), and, opposite, at home in Ripton.

Bound Away
Now I out walking
The world desert
And my shoe and my stocking
Come no hurt.

I leave behind
Good friends in town
Let them get well-wined
And go lie down.

I out think I leave
For the outer dark
Like Adam and Eve
Put out of the Park.

Forget the myth.
There is no one I
Am put out with
Or put out by.

Unless I'm wrong
I but obey
The urge of a song
"I'm bound away!!!"

And I may return
If dissatisfied
With what I learn
From having died.

Robert Frost

For my picture-taker Alfred Eisenstaedt
Sept 25 1958

I am writing this for Alfred Eisenstaedt, whom it has been a pleasure to meet & see at work. *Jacques Barzun, 18.V.56*

For Alfred Eisenstaedt, with admiration and thanks. *Walter Lippmann — May 19.1956 Washington. DC*

To Alfred Eisenstadt my thanks & good wishes *Tennessee Williams May, 1956*

Walter Lippmann, political columnist, in Washington, 1956.

Tennessee Williams—still pleased with the success of *Cat on a Hot Tin Ro*

Jacques Barzun.

Dec 15, 1958

Dear Eisie!
This is a day I shall long
remember. The Weather was Chilly
but the Spirit was Warm.
Your Artistry is exceeded only
by your kindness and goodness.
Hope you don't catch Cold!
Best to You.
Hubert H.
Sincerely
Joan Sutherland

Senator Hubert H. Humphrey in the hat Premier Nikita Khrushchev gave him.

Jan 28/59

Eisie, Dear Eisie —
The first time
was 1936 — the
second 1941 — the
third 1957 and
now, after all these
years I'm still smiling
for you and at you
with love and deep
admiration —

Joan Sutherland with her conductor husband, Richard
Bonynge, after the premiere of *Lucia di Lammermoor* at
the Metropolitan Opera House, 1961.

Gypsy Rose Lee, striptease queen and subject of the musical *Gypsy*.

Darius Milhaud at a music class at the University of Iowa.

Composers Samuel Barber (*Adagio for Strings*) and Gian Carlo Menotti (*The Medium* and *The Saint of Bleecker Street*),1958.

for all your sincerity and kindness to me, I thank you so very much. Also, I had so very much pleasure being with you in our hectic and very satisfying "International episode." My warmest wishes and gratitude - always -

May 17, 1958

Van Cliburn with Steinway staff, 1958.

Gregor Piatigorsky.

Lucille Ball, newly married to Gary Morton.

Noël Coward caught between acts at Sherry's Bar.

Opposite: Angela Lansbury (barefoot) with Joan Plowright in *A Taste of Honey*, 1960.

Elaine May with Mike Nichols in 1960.

Berlin's Mayor Willy Brandt with Arthur Watson of IBM, later American Ambassador to France, 1959.

Nelson Rockefelle

Mayor Robert Wagner.

Thanks again for all their interesting round.

Nelson A. Rockefeller

Pocantico Hills June 1960

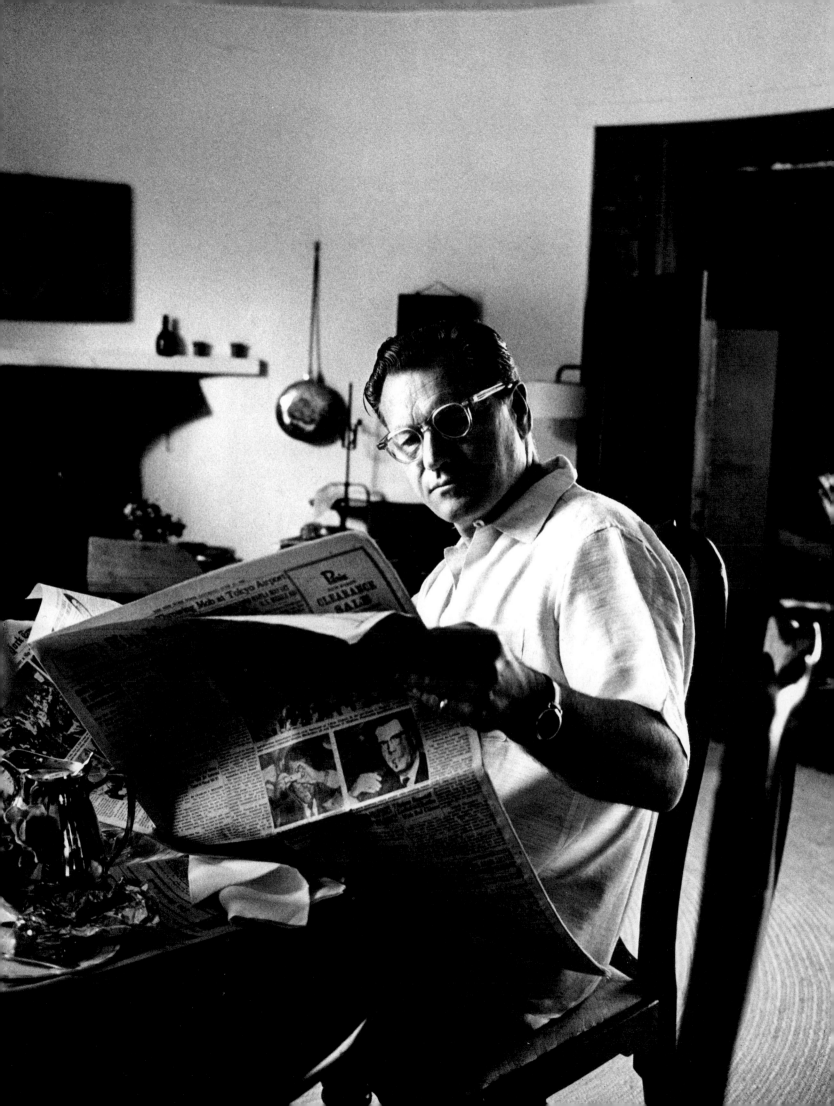

Douglas Dillon, Kennedy's Secretary of the Treasury, 1961.

To Alfred Eisenstaedt
An exceptional Creative Artist
God Bless
Billy Graham
Psalm 16:11

Billy Graham.

To Alfred Eisenstaedt,

In appreciation for his artistic skill, his gentle patience and good humor — the essentials of a great photographer.

Feb '61   Douglas Dillon
Washington, D.C.

Adlai Stevenson, U.S. delegate to the U.N., 1961.

With my thanks to
Alfred Eisenstaedt —
          a great photographer —
     for his gentleness &
     patience —

                    Adlai E Stevenson

With admiration
Robert F Kennedy
Attorney General
Feb 1961

Robert Kennedy looking through my album.

John F. Kennedy

For Alfred Eisenstaedt
who his little artist
makes it both
easy — to too esteem

John Kennedy

I agree!   Elegance

1960

Jacqueline Kennedy, 1960.

OVERLEAF: Mrs. Kennedy with Caroline

Birgit Nilsson as Delilah.

Charles Munch

Thank you very
much for wonderful
work together
with best wishes
yours

Birgit Nilsson

Charles Munch leading the Boston Symphony Orchestra.

BRAVO!

Leopold Stokowski

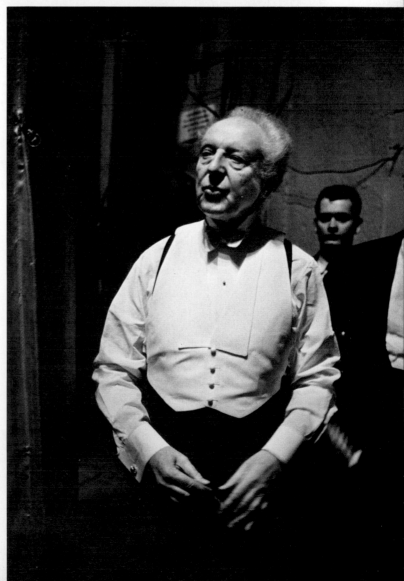

Leopold Stokowski, guest-conducting the Philadelphia Symphony Orchestra.

To Alfred Eisenstaedt
con viva
ammirazione

1964

God bless you for
being such a
wonderful artist
and such a
marvellous human

Sophia

Carlo
Rome 1964

Sophia in London.

OPPOSITE: Sophia in *A Countess from Hong Kong*, the 1966 film directed by Charl Chaplin. Marlon Brando played opposite he

Joseph Wood Krutch, whose *The Voice of the Desert* was a best seller in 1955.

Sigurd Olson, the author and naturalist, near Eli, Minnesota, 1961.

Rachel Carson at the time she was writing *Silent Spring*.

For Alfred Eisenstaedt,
a fellow naturalist, with
the wish that your assignments
may take you always to the
earth's most beautiful spots
Rachel Carson

Roger Tory Peterson, field-book author and illustrator, drawing a young
osprey along the Connecticut River. Three days later it flew from its nest.

To Alfred Eisenstadt

In remembrance of a July
day with the ospreys at Old Lyme
Connecticut.

It was a delight to see
the master photographer at work!

With my admiration —

Roger Tory Peterson

July 1961

Andrew Wyeth (seated) with artist son Jamie in Cushing, Maine, 1965.

Robert Graves at his home in Deyá, Majorca, 1962.

To Alfred Eisenstaedt —
A friend for more
than a quarter of a
century — one of the greatest
artists in the whole
century, with affectionate
regards
Clare Boothe Luce
Phoenix, St. Valentine's 1964

Henry Luce took this photograph of me
with his wife, Clare Boothe Luce, in 1962.

The greatest art of a
good cameraman is invisible try
Eisenstaedt comes well with
this test..
Robt Graves
Deyá
Mallorca

Charlie Chaplin
Feb. 1966.

Charlie Chaplin.

Louis Ferdinand, Prince of Prussia, on horseback
t Burg Hohenzollern, Germany.

Herrn Alfred Eisenstaedt
dessen Meisterschaft uns
tief beeindruckt hat wün-
schen wir von Herzen alles
Gute. Er wird uns immer
ein lieber und willkomme-
ner Gast sein.
      Kira
            Prinzessin von Preussen

*Louis Ferdinand
Prinz von Preussen.*

*Burg Hohenzollern
      im Mai 1963.*

alking with Princess Kira and the caretaker in the courtyard of
he castle. Louis is the grandson of Kaiser Wilhelm II.

Akihito

Michiko.

Japan's Crown Prince Akihito with Princess Michiko.

Marlon Brando.

If "there is no art
to find the minds construction
in the face" you have, perhaps,
have helped importantly
to give it life.

Sincere regards,

Marlon Brando

London, February 1966

Rosalind Russell in Los Angeles, 1965.

Opposite: Joel Gray in the musical *George M*.

with best wishes from
an admirer —

Barry Goldwater

Barry Goldwater, Republican Presidential contender, campaigning in 1964.

Senator J. William Fulbright, Chairman of
the Senate Foreign Relations Committee.

To Alfred Eisenstaedt
whose photographic
genius always
amazes me —
with best wishes from
his friend

Rich Nixon

To a skilled
patient man
of art
Alfred Eisenstaedt
with best wishes
Everett M Dirksen
— US Senate
March 9 1961

Senator Everett Dirksen with Richard M. Nixon in 1961

Pierre Boulez, conducting the New York Philharmonic Symphony Orchestra.

Lorin Maazel rehearsing in 1967.

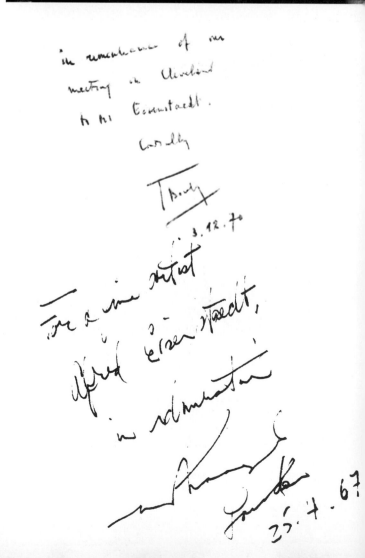

in remembrance of our
meeting in Cleveland
to his Eisenstaedt.
cordially

Truly
3.12.70

For a nice artist
Alfred Eisenstaedt,
in admiration

25.7.67

Colin Davis of the BBC Orchestra going over a score with Yehudi Menuhin.

"To Alfred Eisenstaedt, who knew me when I was too young!
Yehudi Menuhin
London April 29

Only you could have photographed my son & I in the bath!

Colin Davis

Conductor Seiji Ozawa in Toronto.

Vice-President Spiro Agnew.

To Alfred Eisenstaedt
Who has more
patience than a
surgeon dentist

Spiro T. Agnew
Washington D.C.

Nixon's secretary, Rose Mary Woods.

Best wishes
Rose Mary Woods
May 1, 1970

Martha Mitchell.

with fond memories of a
day in October, 1960 in Ohio
when you were Taller Than
I was — with the help
of a friend — you haven't
changed a bit.
John D. Ehrlichman
Sincerely
John Mitchell

John Ehrlichman, Nixon's domestic affairs adviser, and, below, Attorney General John N. Mitchell with Deputy Attorney General Richard G. Kleindienst in 1970.

Ronald C. Ziegler (signature)

Ronald Ziegler, Nixon's press secretary.

Charles (Chuck) W. Colson, Nixon's special counsel.

H. R. (Bob) Haldeman, White House chief of staff.

Very best wishes
Bob Haldeman
May 20 1970

Glad I am joining
your Gallery – Best
wishes & thanks
Chuck Colson
Special counsel to
the President
April 29, 1970 –

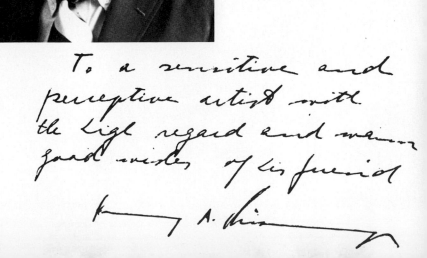

To a sensitive and
perceptive artist with
the high regard and warm
good wishes of his friend
Henry A. Kissinger

Secretary of State Henry Kissinger in the White House barber shop, 1972.

To Alfred Eisenstadt
With appreciation and
with memories of the easiest
& most pleasant session
I've known —
    Best Regards
    Ronald Reagan

Ronald Reagan, California's Governor, 1970.

Melvin Laird, Nixon's Secretary of Defense.

What good company
you keep! And —
manisestes — getting
better & better!

    — My regards & admiration.

Apr 11 '69 .... Wm C Buckley

I am awed
at joining such distinguished
company — just as I
have been awed at
your infinite patience in
trying to bring three
generations of Buckleys
before your camera at
one time —
    Best wishes —
    James L. Buckley
    11/27/70

Opposite: The Buckley family in Sharon, Connecticut.
Seated, left to right: Mrs. William F. Buckley, William,
Carol, and (standing) James, Priscilla, Jane, John, and
Reid.

With love –
Christina Ford –

Henry Ford II in Dearborn.

Mrs. Henry (Christina) Ford at home in Grosse Point.

We have watched
and enjoyed your great
work over many years.
It is always a pleasure
to be photographed by
you – no nonsense –
plus the pictures are
just great – with all
good wishes
Henry Ford

Edwin Land, inventor of the Polaroid camera system, with members of his private laboratory in Cambridge, Massachusetts.

John J. McCloy, U.S. High Commissioner for West Germany and, later, chairman of the board of the Chase Manhattan Bank.

I have had a good many photos taken of me from time to time but this was the least painful experience I have ever had — and it was evident throughout that I was in the hands of one who knew his business.

Jno J McCloy

Chairman —

The Chase Manhattan Bank

To Alfred Eisenstaedt with my best wishes

Erté, artist, fashion designer, author.

Svetlana Peters

Stalin's daughter, Svetlana Alliluyeva Peters, with her husband, Wesley, in Frank Lloyd Wright's house at Taliesin West, Arizona, 1971.

Dr. Christiaan Barnard, who performed the first successful heart transplant in Capetown, South Africa.

Remember there is nothing better than the best

Best wishes

Chris Barnard

Frank Lloyd Wright's widow, Olga Lazovich Wright, at Taliesin West, 1971.

Frank Lloyd Wright in an earlier (1956) photograph taken at Taliesin North, the Wrights' summer residence in Spring Green, Wisconsin.

Take the science of Life in your stride as the mechanics of the affair —
Art and Religion are the essences of being — cultivate them — They are the payoff "—
Frank

To Mr. Eisenstaedt — the master of his work whose unquenchable thirst for creative expression makes him brilliantly young.

Frank Lloyd Wright
Taliesin West
Feb. 23rd
1971

Vladimir Horowitz rehearsing in Cleveland.

Tom Wicker, *New York Times* political columnist, in 1971.

David Rockefeller of the Chase Manhattan Bank speaking
at Harvard University commemorative exercises.

Opposite: Robert Evans, Paramount Pictures production chief, and Barbra Strei
sand discussing the filming of *On a Clear Day You Can See Forever,* 1968

Janet Flanner, the "Genêt" of *The New Yorker*'s "Letter from Paris."

Janet Flanner

Eliot Janeway

Oh, Alfred —
I've been waiting for
you for so long —
I'm just happy that
you have had the
chance to practice
on so many people
before me!
love,
Cloris Leachman

July 16, 1975

Economist Eliot Janeway with his
novelist wife, Elizabeth, in 1975.

Cloris Leachman of *The Last Picture Show* and TV's *Phyllis*.

Please come over and photograph the Irish — if you can persuade them to sit still for long enough!

Desmond Guinness

Desmond Guinness, President of the Irish Georgian Society, with his latest book, 1975.

Neil Simon with his actress wife, Marsha Mason.

To be photographed
by the best in the world
is a supreme honor.
With great admiration,
Neil Simon

To Alfred Eisenstadt,
in grateful appreciation
of your contribution to
our society and with
congratulations on your
superior excellence in
a real art.
Warmest personal best
wishes.
Jerry Ford
December 197-
Washington, D.C.

David W. Rintels under the poster of his new show.

President Gerald Ford.

Andre Previn and Mrs. Previn (Mia Farrow) with their five children on Martha's Vineyard.

The only man who can discuss
Prokofiev and take pictures of five
children at the same time!!
With my admiration and Thanks —
Andre Previn

Mia, above, in 1974, and, opposite, with her "Peter Pan" haircut in 1975.

come back next year
its always good to see
my friend — love Mia Farrow

*grately and
cordially
Thornton Wilder*

Thornton Wilder, 1975.

*All good wishes indeed
and much appreciation
from a Subject.

Olivier
1975*

Sir Laurence Olivier on a
day off during the filming
of *The Marathon Man*.
(See also page 225.)

*we exchange
impressions*

Arthur Miller with his
wife, Inge Morath, just
after finishing their second book together—*In the
Country*.

*As a Photographer's husband I
can appreciate the ancient prayer—"Let
There be light — the right kind." With
love and very best wishes,

Arthur Miller*

The editorial board of *The New York Times,* September 1974: left to right, Herbert Mitgang (standing), Leonard Silk, James P. Brown, Robert Bendiner, Roger Wilkins (standing), Ada Louise Huxtable, Graham Hovey, Fred Hechinger (with pipe), A. H. Raskin, and John B. Oakes.

The Duke and Duchess of Kent.

— Who has helped shape the world and the way we see it with his sensitive and talented eye — and who is still "one of the boys."

With gratitude —

Ada Louise Huxtable

Opposite: Ada Louise Huxtable, architectural editor, in front of her favorite New York high-rise, the Seagram Building on Park Avenue.

Teatime at the Kanins'—Gars[on] with his wife, Ruth Gordon.

Below: The world's greatest ban[k] robber and jail breaker: Willi[e] Sutton, 1975.

Willie Sutton

An honor to be with us this book,

Ruth Gordon

For that one-and-only Eise and his spectacular eye = with admiration bordering on awe!

Garson Kanin

Opposite: The "21" boys—Pete Kriendler, Jerry Berns, and Sheldon Tannen, outside their famous club in New York.

Ansel Adams.

Affectionately

Ansel Adams

You have given so much
to so many of us - Through
your sensitive eye
and generous heart -
To you my deep admiration,
respect and thanks for
a meaningful friendship.
The world would be
greatly diminished
without you.
Your friend
Gordon Parks
April 1974   New York

Gordon Parks, photographer, poet, novelist, film director,
with his wife, Genevieve Young.

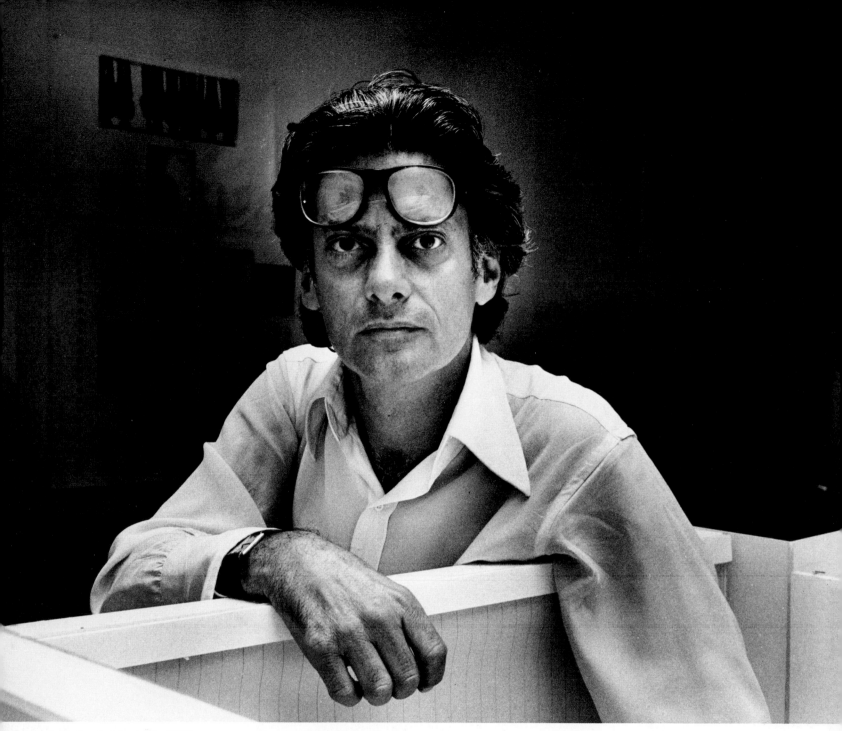

Richard Avedon in his studio, 1975.

Thank you, Eisie,

Avedon.

Beverly Sills

flattered to be
shot by one of the
best
Bill Styron
8/26/75

Beverly Sills during her favorite *entracte*—by the sea.

William Styron also reads what other people write. With his daughter Alexandra.

Lillian Hellman, the summer she was working on *Scoundrel Time*.

For Alfred Eisenstedt —
Who was so patient
with my wiggling children
on Squibnocket Beach —
Shirley Ann Grau

Jerome Wiesner, President of M.I.T.

Vance Packard, author of *The Status Seekers,* at Chappaquiddick.

Jerry Wiesner

For Alfred Eisenstadt —
Who I have admired for
many years. Finally in 1975
I am greatly honored to be
Photographed by him.
Vance Packard

Shirley Ann Grau, Pulitzer Prize winner for *The Keepers of the House.*

To Alfred Eisenstadt —
The fastest legs in the business

CLICK

CLICK
CLICK

CLICK

Many
thanks,
JULES
FEIFFER
7-4-75

Jules Feiffer, while finishing his play *Knock Knock* in 1975.

Left: Kerry Melville and, above, Billie Jean King at Wimbledon, 1971.

Below: Rod Laver and Tom Gorman.

Arthur Ashe winning the men's singles, Wimbledon, 1975.

With admiration,
Art Buchwald
aug 26, 1975

Art Buchwald is "passionate" about tennis.

Above: James "Scotty" Reston, columnist of *The New York Times* and publisher of *The Vineyard Gazette.*

In friendship . . .
Mike Wallace

Below: Mike Wallace, CBS reporter for *60 Minutes*, loves tennis, too.

Walter Cronkite, also of CBS, won a match against Reston.

To 'Eisie'
the one and only.
Better late than never!

Wyatt Cooper and Mrs. Cooper—Gloria Vanderbilt—dressed for a party.

Lilli Palmer, who wrote of her life on stage and off in *Change Lobsters—and Dance*.

Lilli Palmer
Oct. 18th 75

To
Alfred Eisenstaedt
with homage

with love
Gloria Vanderbilt
february 1974

Marthe Keller, the lone feminine star of *The Marathon Man*, in which Dustin Hoffman and Sir Laurence Olivier are also featured. (See also page 209.)

Sophia Loren with her husband, film producer Carlo Ponti. Paris, 1976.

To the best
photographer and
to the dearest
friend —
much love Sophia
Carlo
Paris. Jan 76